Beating Black Kids

So What Have You Been Beat With?

By Asadah

Beating Black Kids

By Asadah

Published by:
Asadah Sense Consulting
New York, New York
www.beatingblackkids.com

Asadah Kirkland, Publisher
Nicole H. Lemon, Editor
Yvonne Rose/Quality Press, Production Coordinator
Fiyahrootz Marketing - Interior and Cover Designer
The Printed Page, Design Coordinator

ALL RIGHTS RESERVED

No part of this book may be reproduced or transmitted in any form or by any means – electronic or mechanical, including photocopying, recording or by any information storage and retrieved system without written permission from the author, except for the inclusion of brief quotations in a review.

Beating Black Kids books are available at special discounts for bulk purchases, sales promotions, fund raising or educational purposes. Call: 646-359-6605 for information and orders.

Copyright © 2009 by Asadah Sense Consulting
ISBN #: 978-0-9836205-9-4

This book is dedicated to all the little souls who only want to be understood and never want to be attacked.

20 NOV 14

Carson!

Thank you for supporting this work!

Love,
Asadah

LOOK IT UP

I put a small glossary (dictionary) in the back of the book. There are words we sometimes think we know, but do not know fully. Be sure to take a look at the glossary and do not pass words you do not understand. The glossary is here to help you. Although you may know a word like "putrid" I put it in the glossary so you can have a clear meaning. WORD!

Table of Contents

LOOK IT UP iv
INTRODUCTION vii
Who Are They? 1
Pass the Baton 4
You Got Chosen 7
Objects 9
Lazy Bones 12
First Exposure 16
Feelin' It 18
Marks 20
Energy 24
Spare the Rod 26
Reactions 30
Shut Down 36
It Don't Work 40
Empty Words and Threats 42
Who's Got Skills? 45
Clothes, Food and a Roof 49
What's in a Word? 51
Unplay the Messages 54
Planned Parenthood 57
All About Me 60
Parent Power 62
Fear 65
Non-Stop Love 67
No Time Out 70

Table of Contents

Got Talk?	72
The Look	76
Pleasure Moments	78
What Do They Want?	81
Love to Hear Them Laugh	84
Let 'Em Live	85
Create It	87
Glossary	90
Author Bio	

INTRODUCTION

I wrote this book because my peers see beating their children as a good solution to handling problems. Some feel beating is okay to do sometimes but not all the time. Some see it as a last resort. Others use beating as a tactic to scare children into good behavior, while others just see beating children as a regular run-of-the-mill response when the kids are driving them crazy!

Well, I never saw beating a child solve the real problem. I have seen beating momentarily make children change their behavior, but I have never seen it make them better. The reason for beating children stems from something else. Perhaps the reason can be traced all the way back to slavery and our relationships with our children then. Who is to say? We have to look at our own choices and why we do what we do.

This book explores why beating was and continues to be typical in the Black community. It challenges us to change our behavior and offers tips on how we can do that. Beating Black kids is controversial. It has been happening for a long time and is very accepted in our culture. Many of us laugh it off as adults, but does spanking do what we say it does when we do it? Is it masking something else?

It is time to look at who children are, what they can do and how beating them affects who they become. Many ideas will come together as a result of reading this book. The goal, though, is to get us to look at how we view

Introduction

children, to stop mentally and physically beating them and to decide where we can go from here.

When you see a 🗝, that means what you are reading is a key that can open up a door to something positive. We are responsible for the adults our children will become. What will we do to fill the world with empowered people who can make good decisions? Read this book and let's decide.

Who Are They?

This book is not about the little people we see as children. It is about the future. All children grow to be adults. They all have feelings. They all have ideas. They all have personalities. They all look for guidance. They are all a responsibility to someone. They are open to change. They are forgiving. They are active. They see a lot. They can plan. One of the things that makes children wonderful is that they can be shaped into the good things we want. They are a product of their environment.

The main thing I try to remember as a mother is that my children are human beings and they are lifetime friends. I try to cultivate them and give them positive energy so that in return I can get the same thing. I try to show them what it is that brings me joy and I try to help [them] to see what brings them joy and then try to get them to respond to other people as they would like the people to respond to them. Constantly reinforcing that creates the energy that is necessary for us to have a good, healthy self, a good, healthy family, community, state, globe and so on.

>**Kandase K.,**
>***Mother of six home-schooled children,***
>***Chicago***

How do we want our future to look? Who is going to create it? Our children can have enough courage and determination to create something big. What if our parents knew to plan our steps? What if they asked and listened to what we wanted to contribute to the world? How would our lives have been different? How early could we have made a change in the world?

Some people start conversations with their children when they are in the womb. Some of us have conversations with our children before they can even talk. These children are asked about their ideas. They are asked about how they see things around them. They are listened to. They are talked WITH.

What about Pranav Veera, the six-year-old genius? What about Latoya Hunter, who wrote a book and toured the country when she was just eleven years old? What about Tyra Banks' mom who managed the first seven years of Tyra's career? For some reason, their parents saw them as valuable to society and listened to their dreams. That means they were watching. Watching a child usually means that instead of making time to beat him or her, a parent is finding resources to push the child's dream further.

A child's contribution to the world does not have to come hard. Struggle does not have to be involved. There is nothing wrong with things being easier for them. Easier feels good and can have great value if we have the skill as adults to create it.

Our children will populate the world in the future, as adults. There is no denying that. What kind of adults will they be is the question. As parents, we influence the answer. Will we put them in a corner or give them the opportunity to decide on something? Will they remember our beatings or will they remember our wisdom?

Who Are They?

❦ Get their advice on something. Ask them some questions. Help them notice the clouds move—literally. Help them see things in life they would not normally take notice of. Give them some of your time. You may be pleasantly surprised to see what they have to offer.

Pass the Baton

Beating Black kids is a passed down phenomenon. I could end the chapter here, but there is so much more to be said and by so many. I believe that Black people beat children because many of us were beat when we were young. It is what we know. Some people don't like the word "beat." Yeah okay. You can call it spanking, popping or whatever you choose, but the point is that our kids are being physically hit when they do something that is not to an adult's liking. The main problem is that hitting has become a solution to getting a good result. Most "spankings" come because a parent wants a child to be doing something better, right? Well, this book is going to look at how much hitting someone really helps.

"Growing up I personally believed that physical punishment was appropriate. That's how I was raised because my parents used to do that to me; mainly my father. That's just how he is in general. I always felt like if that's the only way you can get to a child, then hey, so be it. But then I thought about it and began talking to friends and got exposed to a different aspect of things. I have friends from different backgrounds who have different views on it.

One of my friends spoke to me one day about disciplining kids physically and was just like, "Every time you disagree with friends, do you hit them?" I was like, "No." She said, "What's the difference? If you have the need to beat children if you disagree with them, then it is sort of like you're bullying them to an extent, because they are young and they are small and they don't really know better." It's like you'd be more justified hitting the adult because of the fact that they should know better, but like you're hitting a child. Most likely they may not know better, but even if they do know better, it's still the fact that you're this big adult figure and they are just like a little kid. You're hitting them out of anger. You may want to think twice about it before you want to lash out and hit a kid.

Just thinking about it from that perspective, I feel that there should be other ways that you can discipline a child that don't involve you hitting them. I feel like if you raise a child correctly, where they respect you, you won't ever have to hit them. It doesn't matter if you've grown up in a poor background or a rich background, I feel like if you start young with certain things, you won't have to end up spanking the child as a tool to get them to listen to you.

Herbert B.
Youth Advocate, New York

Beating Black kids is done so instinctively that I have not really heard much against "spankings" in our community. But the notion of a grown person striking a child because he or she has misbehaved can seem sort of insane if you just look at it. Where does that response to hit someone when you both disagree come from? Some people allude to where it comes from in the chapters to come. No matter where it comes from, I want us to look at why and when we do it now. Beating Black children is not a practice worth passing down from generation to generation. The only way I see it stopping is if we substitute the behavior with something that actually works. Let's read on and see what we find.

You Got Chosen

I am a firm believer that our children chose us as parents. When I tell my daughter, "I am so glad you chose me as a mom," it automatically gives her the upper-hand in the deal. Although she doesn't say much when I say this, I can see that it makes her feel in charge of something and grants her a little more power and importance.

Now what it does for me is a whole other story. When I think about the fact that my daughter chose me, it makes me reflect on my own qualities. Why would she choose me? How do I act? What does she want to learn from me? How is she influenced by me? What do I see in her that is an extension of me?

Looking at this makes me "better-up" my scene. I look at why I would have chosen me for a little more understanding of her. When I look at the total picture, I see that she must have known I was going to raise her to create her own freedom, in addition to giving her freedom. She must have wanted to dance, too. Laughter was probably what she wanted to do and hear freely. Maybe she did want someone who would care for her colon and have her in a vegetarian environment. Maybe she chose her dad because he likes outer-space, can dance and has a spiritual outlook on some things. I look at the good and the bad of who we are as parents. And when I look at the bad, I take the lessons and outcomes and make sure I can see how she can benefit from those, too.

You Got Chosen

🗝 Since we as parents got chosen, let's choose to be good examples of how we would like our children to be.

-8-

Objects

So what have you been beat with?

a wine bottle

bag of onions

electrical cords

slippers

rolled up newspaper

hands

feet

vacuum cleaner cord

spatula

hot spatula

ruler

dog leash

switch (skinny tree branch)

branch from tree

wire hangers

shoes

trophies

walkman

Objects

washing machine cord

2 x 4 wood

belts (straps)

end table

whiffle ball bat

yard sticks taped together with rubber bands on the end

brush

hot comb

ruler

the big belt

doll leg with platform shoe on

combat boot

Dax top

inner tube

switch with leaves

tricycle

kneeling on rice/corn

phonebook

belt wrapped around fist with five inches exposed

coconut switch

heel of a shoe

broomstick

Objects

fly swatter

wooden serving spoon

wet rag

telephone

kneeling on grits

hot wheels track

cast iron pan

flip-flops

Lazy Bones

"Hey so and so, come here."

"Yes, Mom."

"Come here and hand me the remote." It was sitting right there! How many of us have seen the remote sitting about a foot away from our parents and they called us from another room to come and hand them a remote they could have gotten themselves. Good gracious! The remote is only one object, but we have been subject to get all types of things for our parents. And this occurs at any age! There is no limit.

Now the real deal starts when a child expresses that he or she is not ready to come right then, or doesn't want to come at all. Oh Lawd! It can go something like this:

"Hey so and so, come here for a minute."

The child yells, "Yes, Mom!"

Slightly annoyed, mom says, "I said come here!"

"Okay. In a minute!" the child yells back as he watches television.

Angrily, the mom yells, "What?! I said come here!"

With a huff and a puff, the child answers, "Yes?!"

The mother yells, "Didn't you hear me calling you? What's wrong with you? Go on over there and hand me the remote!"

Lazy Bones

Now the child only got yelled at. This is done so often we don't even see this as wrong. We may laugh at it, but the reality is that the parent is too lazy to get up and get her own remote. As an adult, think of how you feel when someone disturbs what you are doing. Now think of how you feel when someone starts yelling at you. Let's take it further.

"Hey so and so, come here for a minute," mom yells.

"Okay, hold on," the child yells back.

OH LAWD NOT A YELL BACK!

The mother yells, "What! I said come here now!"

"Okay," says the child with a time lapse. "Yes?"

"Come here I said."

The child comes closer and says, "Yes?"

SMACK, right across the face.

"Didn't you hear me calling you? You don't come when YOU want to come. You come when I call you. Now hand me the remote!"

Sound familiar? Even if you've never done this or it was never done to you, why is it so familiar? Why did the parent smack the child? It is because he didn't listen, right? It is because he made the mother wait, right? No. It is because the parent is a "Lazybones!" Well guess what:

- No one wants to be disturbed.
- Even though children are young, they have a right to not want to be disturbed.

- Children usually want to do things for their parents and sometimes a little patience can be exchanged for our laziness.
- We as parents may get a little exercise if we just get up and get things for ourselves.
- Children would not have to experience feeling frustrated or attacked if we just handled things ourselves.
- If parents don't hit children, they will have clean hands instead of the reality of smacking someone on their conscience.

Now we were raised to believe that the child was being disrespectful if he or she did not come right away. Why is that? A child should just DO what a parent says with no emotion attached? I'm not feeling that. Maybe it would help to just take a moment to think about how we feel when we are interrupted by someone for a non-emergency. We are annoyed when we're in the middle of something and people expect us to just stop what we're doing. The end result is that we either tell them how annoying they are or we harbor it and hate them later.

The way young people feel is really no different. What they know is that they HAVE to do what the adult says if they want to avoid the violent end result. What we fail to do as adults is consider how they feel. It's not really important to us. They are supposed to just do as we ask when we ask it, because we gave them life. We willingly took part in those nine months, though and the nine months don't justify mistreating the living, breathing

Lazy Bones

children with feelings that sit in the other room. 🔔 Give a little thought to how they feel and the outcome will probably be different. The wonderful thing is that children really come to help out most of the time. Sometimes they just want us to wait a minute or two. It is not a long time to wait, when you look at all the time we have. And besides, doing things for ourselves will do us more good than harm.

First Exposure

What is a child's first exposure to violence? When do they experience it first? Some young people witness violence first hand as young as two years old. First comes the label, "Terrible Twos" or "Bad," and next comes the beatings. When children learn hitting as a way of communicating, it is no wonder that violence becomes their language in school and sometimes for life. Then the street gets a chance to walk on in.

Beating has happened to even the best of us and it has symbolized a way to supposedly get people to do things immediately. It has been used to get a certain result, gain a certain reputation or power over someone. Any way you look at it, beating from someone you love makes beating valid and okay in whatever circles we have seen it in. If my relative hits me, it is the same hit I would give to another person I felt I needed to have power over. If someone hit me as a child to get me to do something, I just may hit someone else to get something.

Hitting may be human nature, but it is the most animal-like behavior we possess. What makes it worse, though, is that animals usually create pain to survive. We create pain because of imbalanced emotions. Are you in your right mind when you strike a child, or are you stressed, angry, tired, restless and just not yourself? Think about it.

First Exposure

Children see domestic violence. If a child sees one parent beating up the other, and the victim remains powerless, the child will more than likely take on the behavior of the person who has the power.

So what's the solution? One possible solution is to find the good things that bring you joy and make them as much a part of what you do as possible! If we are happy, we usually won't take out our frustration on someone else.

We can be aware of how our children respond to things at an early age. We can also think about how we will live on in our children's minds. Many people do think back to the beatings their family members gave them. They will even rationalize why the beating was necessary for them to get. They begin to rationalize the beatings they give to others. No beating feels right or good when you are getting it. So think first before you even begin to do it, and just don't do it.

We can control what our children see and experience. Fighting turns to pain and pain can turn to death. If they see lives can be beaten when they are young, they can see lives as easy to take away when they get older. What role in the violence will we be responsible for?

Feelin' It

When I was younger, I didn't get beat much by my mother because I was pretty much a good girl. My aunt was the one who was impatient and she would beat us for just about anything. But we couldn't scream when we were younger, because we didn't want the neighbors to hear and get offended. So we had to kneel on the floor and put our faces in the mattress as we got spanked, so that we could cry and scream in the mattress and no one would ever hear it.

> **Danielle B.**
> *After School Administrative Assistant, New York*

Have you ever been beat by someone? How does it feel to be punched, kicked, smacked or hit with an object? It is painful. It affects you emotionally. You are left feeling worse. Being attacked is being attacked. It doesn't matter where it comes from; the hitting affects the body the same. Think of your beatings or the beatings of someone you know. How did they feel afterwards? From what I've heard, they often felt hatred. There never seemed to be a feeling that the beating was a result of being loved by someone.

Feelin' It

I know in a certain time, children had no place, no voice and no say in the matter. But we are not in that time anymore. The daily stress and pain is not on us from the "forces that be" to create the same stress anymore. Our children can be better educated now and don't have to grow up and help support the family. We have more skills today. Our children have more ways to learn and communicate today than we did in the past.

As our children have changed, will we change? Our children require more conversation today. Will we give it to them? If we spend our time beating them and creating pain, they will learn from someone or something else. Feeling pain is teaching in action. It is making children either fearful of the attacker or immune to the pain. When our children become immune to the pain, it is possible that they become adults who create pain in other people. It is like they take on the personality of the people who always got things their way. At the point where the pain no longer affects the child, we have to go to a whole other level of disciplining our kids. Verbal communication is pretty sour at that point and getting through to a child can be very hard. What I usually hear from parents is, "I just don't know what to do now!"

Coming up with something better than beating a child early on can help you avoid this. When children have to look forward to feeling pain from some of the people they love the most, the only real thoughts are about the pain. They really are not thinking about how they are going to change for the better.

Marks

Beating someone and leaving marks seems atrocious, but it is real. Many people have stories of welts being left on their bodies after one of their parents beat them. All those marks usually indicate internal or external bleeding. They are constant visual reminders of having been attacked by someone. They usually hurt to the touch and sting when anything is applied to them. Don't just think about the marks you may leave now. Think about the marks left on you or your friends. What emotions did those marks create in you? Most of us felt resentment, hatred, sadness, anger and other negative emotions. The main thing is that we all can identify with not feeling good at all.

Now, children may not repeat the action that got them the beating in the first place, but are they better? When you were beaten, did it make you love your parent more at that time? Did you care for them more? How would you have felt back then if someone helped you understand how what you did impacted other people? Nine times out of ten, what you did was severe only in your parents' eyes, but not yours. Sometimes they just didn't like how your behavior made them look to others. In most cases, the beating stemmed from your parents' reality and not yours.

If real growth and change need to occur in children, then we should find out what is behind their actions. Where did they learn the behavior? Why did they do it? How did it make them feel? How did it make others feel?

For children to open up and even reveal these things, they have to have some trust. Our children will have that trust and want to talk to us if we create that type of communication early on. ♟ It is about not always making them wrong for what they think and feel. It is about listening to what they think and feel, regardless of whether we like it or agree with it or not. The real skill is in how we handle what we hear.

__To beat a child is to kill a soul__. As a child, I was outspoken, inquisitive and active and enjoyed making people laugh. Sure, that sometimes included talking back to adults or disrupting the class, but I never meant to hurt anyone. NEVER! As you can imagine, this caused a lot of conflict for me. Always being sent to the principal's office or home from the after school program or kicked out of activities because nobody had the patience to deal with me. Naturally, at home, I questioned things I was told and would act out against things I did not agree with. As a result, my family beat me until the age of 13. I say my family, because in my family, the children were raised by the WHOLE village! Everyone got a piece of me, but to no avail. My family members tried their hardest to change who I was. The physical pain they caused me did not outlast the emotional and spiritual setbacks that resulted.

As a little person, and then even as a teenager, we looked to adults for guidance and direction, comfort and support and, most importantly, love and acceptance. To physically cause a child pain is not a sign of love. It is what it is: PAIN!

It's more than just a beating. It's invalidation. It's forcing another being to succumb to your command and it's making another person wrong without verification. Its effects are numerous and often overlooked. Its physical effects are short lived, but the mental detriment is long lasting. While adults see a beating as a punishment for a misdeed, a beating for a child is change. It's more than just a reaction to an action, it's outright disgust and disapproval. The interpretation of a beating for a child is not "Oh, but they love me, so it's okay." It's more like "Why don't they like me and what did I do wrong?" It's more than a belt to the bottom and blisters to the arms or bruises to the legs. It's the thoughts of why the beating is happening in the first place that stay with the child, because nobody ever explained to him or her that there was another way to express oneself; another way to fix the problem, another way to make people feel good, another way to be heard!

Although the bruises to the body heal, one cannot take back bruises to the soul.

Tanya J.
Beauty Consultant, New York

I have found that things usually go the way I want them to when I find out from my child all the factors involved in why she did something. I can get her where I need her to be once I am clear on why she did what she did in the first place. I know. Most Black adults do not and will not take the time to do this. Or will we? It is a choice. It only takes the foresight to see what beating the child will create in the long run and what a child who can reason will create in the long run. We shape our children into the adults they become. What are you making? Are you leaving

Marks

marks? 🔑 When we leave our mark, it should be a mark that creates pride, not a mark of pain.

Energy

How many of you have given a child a beating before? Do you remember the amount of energy it took to actually beat the child?

Girl, my mother used to beat me until I almost passed out! In fact, one time she beat me so hard and so long with an extension cord, that I did pass out. It was just crazy. After that I was really angry with her and I didn't speak to her. I was mad at her after that beating. I was twelve years old when I got that beating. After that, when she would beat me again, I would do everything in my power not to cry. I would just let her beat me. She beat me and she wore herself out! I just didn't tolerate the pain anymore. I just wouldn't deal with that. After that, when she saw beatings weren't going to work, she decided she would give me little speeches. When she decided that she'd give me those speeches and she started talking TO me and not AT me, then I released all of my emotions and I cried because I understood what she was trying to convey to me.

Vanessa L.
Digital Photographer, Atlanta

It takes a lot of energy to beat a child. The physical end result is usually the huffing and puffing of the adult, because of the constant up and down motion of a slapping or punching hand. One woman told me about how tired she was from trying to beat her daughter (she didn't know why she was beating her in the first place). Some may not agree that a lot of physical energy is used up, because they

Energy

get in, get on and get out with their beatings. So let me touch on the mental energy consumed when attacking young people.

The mental energy we will use up before we beat a child is incredible. Our thoughts become full of justifications for beating the child. And after we beat the child, we justify his or her welts and bruises. Somehow we convince ourselves that the beating is going to help the child in the long run.

When you sit back and think of the state of children after they get a beating, where do you think they are emotionally? Are they better or worse off? When you were given a beating, at the time of the beating were you better or worse off? Although beating MAY prevent the child from repeating the behavior that got him or her into that mess, we have to ask ourselves if the resentment and bad feelings are worth it. Depending on how we show our love or whether love is something we do, this feeling may or may not be important to us. If the child is admired by the parent, the beating will be hard to muster up. If we admire our children, we'll spend less time designing their beating and more time trying to find out why they did something we did not approve of. And then we will work to fix it. There is always an underlying reason. The question is whether or not we have the patience and skill to find out what that reason is.

Spare the Rod

"Spare the rod, you spoil the child." Who wrote that? Yeah I know we can find it in Proverbs 13:24, but who wrote that? I never heard of Jesus beating children with rods. I never heard of Jesus beating children at all. I also do not know how the person who wrote that line in the Bible treated his child. I just cannot see how anything a child does could warrant being beat with an object.

"I became a "born-again" Christian in my early 20's and was still new to learning my new faith when my two daughters were young. At the time, I was working overnight at a New York City law firm as a legal word processor and was very indoctrinated in biblical scripture. One night I came into work and an attorney requested to have on hand a word processor and a proofreader outside his office. My supervisor selected me as the word processor and a coworker who was of the Rastafari faith as the proofreader. Rastafari also relies on biblical scripture, but usually for metaphoric purposes and not literal meanings. He told me that he had seven children and we got on the subject of forms of discipline. You see, based on my religion, I was not only encouraged by the church to utilize corporal punishment as a means of discipline, but sat in sermons that preached that if you spare the rod, your actions are ungodly and sinful, because you are not raising your children correctly. Therefore, I promoted this outlook in the conversation I had with my coworker. He told me that he felt corporal punishment was not godly and that he never laid a hand on his seven children. I then proceeded to say, "But the Bible says..." and he politely

Spare the Rod

stopped me to ask me a question. "When you think of a rod, what do you think of?" I said, "Well, I think of a sturdy, dense stick." And he said, "Right, something that doesn't bend or break even when hitting something with it." I said, "Yes." And he said, "Now how do I look beating my child with something like that." And I said, "Yeah, but..." and he continued, "The Bible can be full of wisdom if taken in the right context. When I read 'rod' in that scriptural text, I applied the same qualities of a rod to myself. I became the rod. I was sturdy, firm and I did not break or bend. When I said 'no,' my children didn't test or question it, because they knew they couldn't 'bend daddy'." I never forgot that conversation, because he passed so many jewels to me. I was so moved by it. I did have a problem with consistency with my children, but realized that consistency is the "key" or the "rod" that you must not spare.

Fiyah
Web Designer, Atlanta

Most people do not know about how "the rod" in scripture got mistranslated. In Coptic Christianity, from Ethiopia, where Christianity derived, "the rod" referred to the healing rod. It was two-pronged and when tapped on someone with good health, it would vibrate a lot. When tapped on someone with poor health, it would vibrate less. If you spare THAT ROD you spoil the child because he then would not be fully healed. Thanks to the scholar in Philadelphia that led me to that wonderful piece of history. Makes much more sense doesn't it!

Spare the Rod

Now when I think spoiled, I think rotten, putrid or unable to be eaten. How could a child be any of these things? I have seen children highly loved. This is not to be mistaken for being spoiled. I am not talking about the children who have no order and who get things bought for them all the time either. Their "out of orderness" is a result of adults who are not meeting their true needs. If a child is not beat, does what he or she wants and gets everything, you can call the child spoiled if you want. I prefer to not get all caught up in titles. We just have to get to the root of why the child is causing problems. His or her problems are stemming from some other something and that something is the parents a lot of times. Do the looking. No judgment here; just look.

My concern is that we get upset about a child receiving a lot of love. I have had people ask if my child is spoiled. Of course I give them the definition of spoiled. But more than that, I tell them that my daughter is simply highly loved. She has manners, she is aware of how most of her actions affect others and she makes people feel good overall. I do not beat her. I do not have to. I get what is desired by talking to her and weighing things out. Because of the way we communicate, I usually only have to say things once. When she cries, I comfort her, because my goal is to have her experience positive things. Even when her crying comes from my disapproving words, I still comfort her. Getting her to calm down is the only way I will hear her side and the only way she will hear mine. I want her to see me as a person in her life she can trust. Hate and resentment are not the emotions I need her to feel towards me. I am very aware of the type of person I would like to offer you all in her. Even if all her decisions are not to my liking, I still value and guide her as a child. No rod will ever be used to prove a point to my daughter. Beating her would not make her powerful. It would only make her possibly fear me and, eventually, the world she lives in.

Reactions

What was your reaction, knowing the hurt was on its way? You can find descriptions of the behavior of beaten people at most abuse agencies. Reactions to beatings are important, because a person is being created when the beating is done. There are a lot of negative visual and mental memories to bear. I am only going to make a list of what I have seen and heard. I want you to do your own looking.

Children experience being beat in various ways. They may:

scream

be embarrassed

have less love for the people who beat them

have less respect for the people who beat them

be sad

be angry

be less willing to do things

be less capable of doing things

be aggressive

be frustrated

have no motivation

be held back

Reactions

be shy

be hurt

be misunderstood

carry bad habits

misbehave

be less involved

stop talking

be bitter

be violent

show no visual sign of emotions they really feel

not be able to reach their goals

have a life full of problems

have plain old embedded feelings that only come out in their actions...if someone is looking

I can only remember two beatings I got from my mother. The others are suppressed in my memory as being chased around the kitchen table, grabbing the belt she was going to beat me with; resulting in a literal tug-of-war or being cooped up in a closet for hours hoping that by the time I came out she would've forgotten all about her threats of sending me back to Haiti and making me mashé S S (a popular term in Kreyol meaning making me walk in S'). This was something I hadn't understood until adulthood when someone explained to me that it meant you'd get a beating so bad that you wouldn't be able to walk in a straight line, but in a series of S's like a drunk.

Reactions

I never did get a beating so bad to make me walk in S's, but I could remember being able to count the welts on my arms and legs from one of those beatings. The first one was when I was five years old. Aside from the stinging pain of the belt hitting against my skin, I was mesmerized at how the welts were different shapes and with the application of warm salt water with a wash cloth, they would shrink and disappear—long before I would stop crying of course. It was one of those beatings where you'd fall asleep and still be whimpering as you slept. I remember my mother trying to soothe me and just a few moments earlier she had accused me of being a thief. She had found a toy in my book bag that hadn't belonged to me and thought that I had taken it from another child. What she didn't know was that most of the other girls in my kindergarten class had Strawberry Shortcake book bags and I had taken the wrong one home. I remember pleading with her trying to let her know that I didn't do it. There's nothing more heart wrenching than being falsely accused.

Like when my mother thought I was enticing the 19-year-old nephew of her new husband when I wrote secret love letters to him in my notebook when I was 10. There were no welts from that beating because I was old enough to know that I could run and dodge the belt. But the inner scars didn't disappear with soothing warm salt water. They lingered and festered and I had to find an outlet to release them, to heal them. My mother had beat me in front of her new husband and older stepdaughter whom I hated and the cute nephew who was embarrassed by the whole thing. I didn't know what she was trying to prove by making it a public scene, but I sure was going to take back my 10-year-old dignity for my sake. So I hid stuff. I'd see house and car keys lying around and I'd hide them. I would hide wallets, money, clothes or anything that I thought was of value to anyone, except for my mother. I didn't hide her things because I still liked her for some reason. I would get a kick out of watching my new stepfather lose his mind looking for his keys and running late for work. I did it because they had watched me get beat and in my own imagination, they were laughing at me. They may have felt some sort of pity or compassion, but they shouldn't have seen that moment between me and my mother.

The beatings, the yelling, and the chastising were all personal moments between us. I knew even at an early age that it was something that my mother and I were working out. What amazes me even now is that I would always forgive her, but I would have a seething hatred at any onlookers. And as I entered my teenage years, the onlookers became just about everybody else. So instead of hiding people's things, I would steal.

In retrospect, I stole because I was trying to take back my power. There's something very demoralizing about a beating, be it physical or verbal. And maybe those beatings had something to do with how I treated my body and the relationships I had with boys. It gave me the sense that my body did not belong to me.

Ultimately, aside from the welts, the onlookers and the emotional scars, what I remember the most are my mother's eyes during the beatings. She would be clenching a belt, a man's belt, breathing heavily and glaring down at me with glazed, wandering eyes. They were not hateful or demonic. Instead, my mother's eyes were weary and full of fear. That's why I forgave her.

I've forgiven her because at some point in her career as a Registered Nurse she learned that there was something wrong about beating a child like that. She

Reactions

must've taken a child abuse class where she was taught to look for bruises on a child who'd come into the hospital and it was her duty to bring it to the attention of officials for suspected child abuse. So she never beat my sister who's eight years younger than me and will tell my mother off in a heartbeat without thinking twice about it. She never beat my little brother. To this day, I'm amazed at how candid and playful he is with the woman I grew up fearing. Both my brother and sister were born here in America; I was born in Haiti. I was raised to have an unflinching fear of adults. I had to not look them in the eye and was obligated to kiss every single adult in a room, even if it was the strange man who always insisted that I sit on his lap. I was from a culture where children were beat with rulers and kneeling on rice grains in a corner was considered a lenient punishment.

And now as I raise my children as veggie burger-eating, budding environ-mentalists who attend progressive schools where teachers and staff are on a first name basis, I get called on by my four- and six-year-old on so much as raising my voice. "We have to speak nicely to our friends," they say. When I tell them in a stern voice that I'm not their friend, I'm their mother, they look at me like I'm crazy. I think I pulled somebody's ear once and it was as if I'd violated her very soul. She cried not from the pain, but from the sense of utter disappointment. At some point, I must've instilled a certain level of dignity and respect because they absolutely do not tolerate anyone putting their hand on them.

Reactions

Indeed, a small victory on my part, because after all, I've managed to break a cycle and heal.

Ibi Aanu Z.
Teen Fiction Writer and mother of three
New York

Shut Down

I have heard, "That technique may work with your child Ms. K, but not with my child!" Yeah, of course not! Your child has gotten beatings before!

Taking time and talking things out may not work with some children initially, because they have gotten beatings a trillion times. Think about it. How often do you converse and confide in the people who have given you beatings?

The issue is the type of people our children turn into after being beat a number of times. They tend to shut down around the people who beat them and have very little to talk about. When someone comes around that will not beat the child and genuinely wants to communicate with the child, it takes more work. Once a child has shut down, I have seen only the skilled be able to get anything out of them.

This is when gaining their trust becomes crucial. If something is bothering a child, my opinion is that he or she should be able to confide in the parents.

Well when I had my first child (even though I raised my younger brothers and sisters) I can truly say it seemed like I knew nothing about having a baby. He cried a lot. I didn't know what to do. I sang. I cried. I was alone with this child. I didn't know what to do and his father thought that he was spoiled and that I held him too much. He had a real problem with this. I guess it was some sort of insecurity or jealousy. I don't know. I can't quite figure it out. I realize now that he was a crazy

Shut Down

man. He would slap this child. The baby was like three or four months old. He would start crying and he would start slapping him. I was so afraid that he was going to hurt him. The baby would just seem to bounce back no matter what. He [my husband] would take him out of my arms sometimes and kind of toss him into the crib and say, "You're spoiling him!" He said I showed favoritism towards him. He was crazy. When my other children came along, he would call my first son all kinds of names. I thought maybe he would change. I don't know why. Looking back on it all, it seemed like I was the crazy one. He didn't change. He got worse.

I called myself spanking my sons (my other children too, but mainly my sons), because they were always "hyperactive." I guess it was the mentality that they were supposed to sit still and be quiet. If they weren't still and being quiet then they were being bad. So they were constantly being physically punished. And then they tore up the house. We didn't realize that all of this "discipline" as we called it, wasn't discipline. It was just outright abuse now that I look back on it. It was people's ignorance. We were ignorant. I was with a man who was of the ultimate ignorance (or craziness) and I didn't do anything about it. I yelled and screamed and got into a lot of fights with him over it. I didn't know what to do.

Our children were at such a disadvantage. They were just being children and constantly being punished for it. It was crazy. In the end, it seemed like the more whippings and stuff the children got, the worse they got.

Shekhinah B.I.
Hair Stylist, New York

Shut Down

Some of the worst things I have come across are young people who have shut down. They become introverted, non-responsive, don't talk, can be sad, unlikable and angry, can be bad listeners, challenging to work with and tons of other things. Many people like to judge young people who are like this. They seldom look at the conditions that came before the shut down. I bet if we looked, we would find some beatings up in there.

To avoid children who shut down and become adults who do not keep healthy relationships, more thought should be given to how children are treated. It is common for people to open up less when they are attacked. They really do not know who to trust and it takes time for them to trust anyone. ❦ So my advice is to stop beating children! Maybe if you stop to think about why you have beaten a child in the past and then work to help the young person understand your moments of insanity and impatience and learn a little more about you, the attacker, then maybe they will switch roles and become a little more understanding. Maybe. Adults are human, too. Understanding us better and why we get upset and stressed can aid a young person's decision making. ❦ Getting more communication going is a key. There's nothing wrong with confiding in young people. I have found them to be extremely caring and concerned once they know us better. Check and see if you may have shut down in life; and if so, why? ❦ Open up a little. Let the truth be your guide.

It does become a little complicated to fix things once a child has shut down. I never said it was easy. But it is

Shut Down

worth fixing if having that child really do well in life is a concern of yours. ♟ Another key is to help children feel free about most things, especially communicating.

It Don't Work

There's not a lot to say here other than "BEATINGS DON'T REALLY WORK!" They sting, they hurt, they leave marks, they may temporarily stop a behavior, but they don't really work. I have heard at least four stories where children, now adults, preferred the beating over punishment because the beating was over faster and they thought punishment did more harm to them. The beatings don't really work because there's no real lesson learned. Both the adult and the child end up feeling worse and growth is never really accomplished. It's WHACK! 'Nuff said!

Beating does not work because the kids get hip to it. My sister and I wanted to kick in my brother's drums. He was the youngest. She's the oldest, I am in the middle and I had attention issues, but that's another story. I was telling my sister that we should kick them in and then he wouldn't be able to play them anymore and we wouldn't have to listen to his horrible playing. She told me that if we did it we were going to get a beating. I told her, "It's alright. After mama hits you five times, cry and then she'll stop. And then she's going to tell us, 'You go in the room, you go in the room. You sit on your bed, you sit on your bed' and then it will be over."

So we did it. My mom hit us five times and we started yelling and we started screaming and we started crying (fake tears) and then she stopped. She told us, "Sit on your bed, you sit on your bed and I don't want to hear

It Don't Work

anything else," and that was the end of it. But the drums were kicked in. And I told my sister, "I told you she was going to stop hitting us."

Vanessa T.M.
After School Program Director
New York

Empty Words and Threats

"Don't let me have to hurt you!"

"Watch your tone!"

"Don't let me have to tell you again!"

"I'ma kick yo' ass!"

"This hurts me more than it hurts you."

"I'ma stomp you."

"Cuz I said so!"

"Don't ask me why!"

"And the next time it will be worse!"

"Go get the belt!"

"Fix your face!"

"Sometimes I wish I didn't have kids!"

"Shut up before I give you something to cry about!"

"What did I say?!"

"I'm doing this because I love you!"

"You better shut up before I give you a REAL reason to cry!"

"Keep it up and watch what I do to you!"

"Don't do what I do. Do what I tell you to do!"

Empty Words and Threats

"You think I'm playing, huh? As sure as my name is — I'ma show you who's the boss around here!"

"You are cruisin' for a bruisin'!"

"Children should be seen and not heard!"

"Would you like a reason to cry? I can give you one!"

"Excuse me? Did you say something under your breath?"

"My way or the highway!"

"Keep it up, hear?"

"I'm about to beat you like a b*tch in the street!"

"I'll stick my foot up your ass!"

"Don't look at me in that tone of voice!"

"Are you mad? Then you better scratch your ass and get glad!"

"I'm gonna beat you like you stole something!"

"You betta' not cry!"

"I'm gonna beat you like you a grown man!"

"I'm going to beat the black off of you!"

"I brought you into this world and I'll take you out!"

"Fix your face before I fix it for you!"

"I'm gonna punch you in your chest and make your shoulders clap!"

"I'm going to beat your narrow ass!"

"Wait 'til your dad comes home!"

Empty Words and Threats

"So help me God!"
"Don't make me come back there!"
"Didn't—I—tell—you!"
"Wait 'til we get home!"

Who's Got Skills?

There is no pamphlet for raising a child. For the most part, we learn to raise our children through trial and error. Every child is unique and has his or her own set of behaviors and interests. The question becomes who is even caring enough to develop what we see in our children.

Currently, I am a licensed child care provider and I have a family day care in Harlem. Working with children everyday can be a bit challenging, but at the same time this is something I chose to do, so I have to be passionate about it. Kids come in small packages and have different personalities. The way I deal with their personalities is to actually learn the child. Once I learn the child, then I figure out how to deal with him or her on a personal basis.

Children come into this world with no instructions. Once they are in your presence and your environment, the first thing they want to do is gain trust. If they don't gain your trust, they are not going to be compatible with you. That's one thing parents, caregivers or anyone needs to know.

So when children come into the day care, I will sit down with the parents and interview them. The parents and I can communicate and work on being compatible, but it is the child that needs to mesh with the provider. Once I see that the child is actually compatible with me, we can move forward with the enrollment process.

I know a lot of children that come straight from home into day care settings and they are not able to adjust. So you have to know what to do with that child, how to do it and when to do it.

Samantha D., Licensed Child Care Provider, New York

☝ One of the first steps is to see the child as a solution. Everyone has a role to play in this world. President Obama, Martin Luther King, Jr. and Harriet Tubman: these leaders were not necessarily raised by people who knew they would become the leaders they became. And I don't even know what their upbringing was like. What I do know is that if we as parents see leadership qualities and cater to them early on, our children will probably take on leadership earlier and more easily.

Each leader makes life more organized and, sometimes, easier for others. It is no small role. To build a leader takes skills. ☝ To build a leader, we have to:

watch

listen

talk WITH

discover

sacrifice

give time

laugh

research

Who's Got Skills?

validate

make connections

be patient

listen MORE

There are countless other things required to make a child feel important, but this list is a good place to start.

Oh boy does this take time to do! It really takes time when you have more than one child. But if we are going to be wise enough to have children, we are going to have to up our skill level to shape the people we are bringing into the world. When we exercise the skills mentioned above, kids feel like their ideas are worth something and someone cares about their voices. To take time to develop the patience needed to listen to a child means making a choice. ꯹ When we choose to listen to a child and make him or her feel like his or her stories mean something, that interest goes a long way. That interest produces young people who are not afraid to ask adults questions. Some young people may begin to show gratitude and communicate well with others as a result. This can even create little people who think before they speak and keep others' feelings in mind. Children who are spoken with and asked questions about the world tend to look at and contribute to the world they live in.

꯹ My request is that we make the time to care about our children's voices. I understand that we may even zone out a little bit when they are talking, because there is so much for us to be concerned with as adults. But if our children are talking to us, it is important that we acknowledge them.

> "Really? That happened?"
> "Wow, I didn't know that."
> "How was your day?"
> "Wow, you are so smart!"
> "How did you find that out?"
> "You are so helpful."

These words have the potential to validate. They show the child that you're interested and make him or her feel like they are a part of something. Adults love feeling right. Children love feeling right about the things they say and do, too. The first people to make them feel powerful, good and right should be their parents. When they have these feelings, they tend to be less introverted and give more in the long run.

Clothes, Food and a Roof

"I showed them my love by giving them clothes, food and a roof over their heads." I have heard many parents say this. These things should be included in the "parenting brochure." THAT AIN'T ENOUGH! Those are just things parents need to make sure they can provide before they become parents.

I have found that when parents say that, it is usually an excuse for why they did not give love, attention and some of the other important intangible things children should get from their parents. I am not talking about the attention you give when you tell the child what to do every two minutes and watch them so they do not get hurt. I am talking about the love you give when you don't stop the children all the time. Help them DO something instead of stopping them from doing something all the time. If we need them to be quiet, for example, then we can help them understand how their volume is affecting other people. The love I'm talking about includes an unexplained hug or a compliment. It is how the parent makes the child smile.

Clothes, food and a roof are just bare human necessities for living comfortably in this world. We would not hold the title of parent too well if we did not provide these things. However, these things do not fully measure a parent's love.

Clothes, Food and a Roof

⚜ Our children need support and encouragement for their ideas. They need us to listen to their views. They need freedom to make good choices. They do not need our opinion leading the way. ⚜Let them lead and we follow with an awareness of what they are getting into. Providing material things for them is one thing. Providing things that give children the freedom to create their own reality builds the confidence and character needed to run nations.

What's in a Word?

Now physically beating someone does one thing. This chapter addresses how damaging our mouths can be. Beatings can't be felt physically after a period of time. What I have found is that when we use harmful words, those words can stay with a person for a lifetime.

If your child was to copy you and repeat your most common words to him or her, what would they be? Would they be commands?: "Do your homework." "Don't sit there." "Do as I say do." "Stop talking so much." Would you be talking AT your child?: "Didn't I tell you...?" "What are you looking at?" "You're not making any sense." Would it be name calling?: "Come here you dumb..." "You have a big ole head." "You little nigga." Yeah, these are all real words spoken to real children. How do you sound to your child?

🔑 Being aware of what we say to or around children can help shape who they become and how they act. What we say can chip away at their joy or pull them down. We need to think about how what we say is going to affect a child's day, week or life. I have heard adults in my workshops talk about things said to them as children that affect their behavior to this day. Sometimes they never speak up for themselves. Sometimes they can't believe they can successfully do something. The fact is, words can hurt. What hurts is not the word itself, it is the tone and the intention behind the words. When parents are critical of their children and say things without thinking about how they affect their children, they can damage their children's self-esteem.

Some parents may not care and feel they have a right to say what they want because they are the adults, but they need to look at the type of adults they are going to put in the world. Will the adults we create be so used to being told "stop" that they can't "go" and accomplish things? Will our children be so used to commands and being told what to do that they will be adults that only take orders? Or will our children be so used to conversations and have the ability to think and choose for themselves that they will actually come into the world with enough skills to make good choices?

Power can come to people at an early age. 💡 If freedom to think and choose is given early on, then thinking and choosing become regular behaviors. Practicing patterns of abusive behavior can only make the givers and receivers of that abuse feel low. We may have to change "DON'T cross the street when a car is coming" to "Look both ways when cars are coming." We can turn "Be quiet!" into "Listen to the volume of your voice." I have even heard "How about using your inside voice." That's pretty good, too. Instead of telling them our opinion of what they cannot do or will not become, we can listen to them, watch what they are doing and help them grow.

Let's just teach them, man! 💡 One of the keys is to teach in the positive. It is all in our language. That is what the words above are about. If we are aware of the impact

What's in a Word?

we have on our children and how much they actually take in from us, we can teach lessons through consciously talking in the positive and make a major difference in how they behave. We can affect the way they act within the world dramatically. It will freak you out most when you hear them repeat what you have said in their own everyday language. ♟ Teach them to ask questions if they do not understand something. This has made me smarter, because I have to come up with good answers to the questions I am asked.

Children can hear the anger and frustration in our tones. Now when it comes to disciplining, sometimes we do need to put a little force in our voices so they will understand how serious we are or how severe the situation is. ♟ I only ask that we explain why the situation is severe. Children need to understand how their actions are connected to other things. This approach may take more time, but someone's spirit won't be broken in the process.

__Unplay the Messages__

Play it back. What are your first memories of your relationships with the adults in your life? I hope they are positive ones. Some people cannot remember; others have blocked them out. Some memories are sweet and endearing. Some make us laugh; others make us cry.

Well, I wrote this chapter because of my godmother. When I heard her story and actually heard her talk about wanting to "unplay the messages," I knew it was important to pull our coat tails to the madness. My godmother mentioned that she is sixty years old and still experiences the negative effects of her first memories of her mother. Yes, she was given physical beatings as a child, but it has been the verbal beatings that have shaped some of her beliefs and the way she chooses to act as a woman.

My mother used to say to me that I was stupid, even though I made rather good grades in school. She said that I was stupid and so I believed her. When I got to be in my late teens, I talked about going away to school and learning to drive. She told me that I should not think about driving, because I would probably kill somebody or kill myself. To her I wasn't smart enough to operate a car. So here I am, sixty years of age, wanting to relocate and leave New York, but the thing that kind of holds me back from that is the fact that I can't drive. There's a part of me that's still afraid, because of the messages I haven't unplayed from my childhood.

Dale W.T.
Godmother, New York

Unplay the Messages

Who did the mean words serve? Who did they do harm to? You see, my godmother is a good citizen of this world—by choice. She helps many people. This does not negate the fact that what was said to her as a child still creates pain for her as an adult. Had she not been strong and determined, she could have become a very different person. Destruction could have been her way of living; destruction of herself and others.

When we are not aware of how what we are saying gets recorded in a young person's head, we run the risk of raising a person who cannot contribute good things, because he or she has held on to someone else's words and beliefs. Think about it. What have you said to halt your child's actions? What's been said to kill your child's dreams? What can't your child do well on account of things you have planted in his or her head? You see, these messages do not get publicized as roots to our children's problems. They may be vocally unplayed, but they play over and over in their heads for years and potentially become things they believe to be true. So they act on them. Or, they may not act at all.

Our children trust us. What we say to them is usually law. They usually live by what we say and develop their ideas of the world by our words. ⚷ One of the keys is to plant ideas in their heads they can grow from. We can say and plant things that make them happier and wiser. "You want to be a Spanish teacher? Girl, you can speak and learn in all kinds of countries like, Spain, Venezuela and Mexico."

Unplay the Messages

Even I must be very aware of what my daughter is recording. Is she recording a bunch of orders or is she recording something more, something good? She will record what she wants, but it's my job to ensure that the information I give her motivates her to do well.

Planned Parenthood

Ooooh! This topic is a doozy!

Question: How many Black parents actually planned our parenthood? I would be lying if I said I did. I know a few people who did plan. I think that some thought should be given to how we are going to parent before we actually have children. When some thought is given, we think through the trouble spots and figure out how we will come up with solutions.

Thinking about having a child, I thought about my responsibility to that human being. It wasn't about trying to create a perfect being. It had a lot to do with troubleshooting and working out kinks. I knew my daughter would ultimately be a reflection of me and my ability to raise a child. If my child was seen negatively, I would have to look at me and what needed to be fixed in me. If my child made people feel good, I would feel good knowing people would look to me and know that I must have created a child with that ability.

I look at my child now and see that overall she makes people feel good. Now, she's very direct and will speak her mind. When her actions don't make people feel good, I don't beat her. I talk with her. You see, what I know is that she is wise. She has some understanding about how she functions in the world. I understand that she may not always understand how her words and actions make other people feel—even me. So we talk about it.

Planned Parenthood

I have to ask her some questions. You know, get in her mind a little. I don't make her wrong for what she does; I only explain the effects of what she does. I ask her about her choices and if she did or said something to cause the feeling she created in the other person. What I have found is that she usually did not want to make the other person feel bad. Once she gets an understanding of the effect she created, then we look at what she can do to make it better. It is my job to take the time to help her reason. We almost always come up with better results. And my daughter is five years old.

> *One day my wife and my daughter were in my wife's bedroom and they were having a discussion and my daughter was getting verbally disrespectful with my wife. As my daughter exited the bedroom, I stood by the door and held up my hand and she walked directly into it. Her face fit nicely in the palm of my hand and I clenched my fingers tight so her face was locked into the palm of my hand. I then pulled her face close to my mouth and whispered in her ear, "If you ever talk like that to your mom again, I will take skin off your behind. Do you understand me?" Because her face and mouth were locked in the palm of my hand, you just saw my hand motion up and down the same way her face did when she said yes. I explained to her that I wanted her to go back in the room and apologize to her mother and stay in her room because she was on punishment. I then let her face go and she went into the room to apologize to her mom. I got pleasure out of not having to hit her and have her disciplined like that.*
>
> **Rick H.**
> **Head of Maintenance, New York**

Planned Parenthood

℗ So even if we did not plan our children getting here, let's start to plan the remaining time we have to be their parents. They do look up to us. They do want our understanding. They do value our opinion. They do want our moral support. And the list goes on. This requires us to want to give all of that. That's a lot to give; that is a lot of responsibility.

It is faster to beat a child and takes very little skill to do it. But if we are going to be parents that create love a child can feel, ℗ then we will make the extra time to communicate and get to the bottom of the problem. The end result will be parents who feel more accomplished and children who gain understanding from the love and time their parents take to help them reason through something.

All About Me

Many parents beat children because they do not want to be embarrassed. A child is talking loud in public, gets a smack and is told to be quiet. Sometimes it's more than a smack. Many beatings come to children because of how their behavior makes the parent look to others. IT AIN'T ABOUT US! How children act is a reflection of who they are. If we do not want who they are to reflect badly on us, then we need to think about what we are doing and saying to them at home.

My mother had a problem with alcohol my first twelve years and I remember having to drag her as a little girl to the bathroom to throw up. It was difficult. She was angry with herself. She adopted me, but she passed her pain along. She had not been treated well as a child. She was given away by her mother, because she was considered too dark. Her aunt raised her. She didn't grow up in a household where there was a lot of love and nurturing. When she adopted me as an infant, she wanted a child, but she didn't know how to love a child. She had never been loved herself. She was so angry with things not working well in her life and she took that anger out on me.

One of my early recollections is an incident that took place in the complex where I grew up. I was four years old. I was at the foot of the playground and my mother and some other ladies were sitting on the bench right outside. I was talking with some of my friends. I don't remember exactly what my mother said or did, but it was something embarrassing. She may have been loud

All About Me

or cursed, because she did use a lot of profanity. I said to my friends, "Well, you know she's not really my mother, because I was adopted." And my mother came over and smacked me. I was embarrassed and I remember looking around the perimeter of the playground, hoping that somehow or another my natural mother would be there. Even though I had never seen her, I wanted her to come to protect me.

Dale W. T.
Godmother, New York

Are we loud at home? Do children see violence at home? Are our children hearing inappropriate conversations at home? Are all of our children's interests and dreams being ignored at home? Are the changes in our children's interests going unnoticed by us as parents? Getting to the bottom of all of this will help affect a child's behavior in public. If there is some concern for who a child is and what he or she will do in public, ⚷ care about what the child is made up of. This is what will show on the outside. If we want to be seen as better parents, then we have to create good products in our children. Our children can be good role models. We just have to CREATE good role models who care about themselves and how they are connected to other people.

Parent Power

Being a parent gives us power to have and do some things. A parent is one who gives birth to or nurtures and raises a child. Many of us did not consciously choose parenthood; it chose us! If you did not choose parenthood, then the parenting has been big-time trial and error.

This chapter is about our power as parents. How do we get it? My main issue with the power we put out as parents is how we use that power when it comes to the lives we bring into the world.

I can truly say the whipping did not help my children. It didn't make them better people. Instead it made them very angry people, determined to do whatever they wanted to do. All the things that we tried to save them from are the very things they sought out to do. Now when I see people outside hitting their children or yelling at them or putting fear in them, it irks me to no end. It's like I almost feel [their children's] pain in my stomach. I can't stand it. My mother used to whip my brothers. She thought she was doing a good thing too, because her grandmother whipped her brothers—and "whipping" is putting it nicely. It was outright abuse. Older people were using the power they had over their children to just abuse them because they were angry.

Shekhinah B.I.
Hair Stylist, New York

To me, parenting is about ensuring the safety of the child, while he or she is here on this earth. ♀ It is about learning about myself from a different point of view. I can see some of how I act through my child's actions. How smart my child is and how well or not she can communicate helps me see my skill level. As a parent, I do not rule her. It is not my job to tell her what to do just because she is my child. Sure, as a parent I ask my child to do different things. Sometimes she does those things out of protest with a huff and puff. What is important to me is how I react to her response. I do not tell her she HAS to do anything "because I am her mother." I tell my daughter she can choose to do one thing or not, because it is her life. I make sure she understands the meaning of "life" and any other word I use, and I emphasize that the decision she makes will determine what happens next.

Now if I really don't want to have a bad experience as a parent and my daughter wants to do something that I see will also affect ME negatively, I talk about that, too. If she wants to eat cheese, which will make her a congested mess, I explain to her that her runny nose, swallowing mucus, clogged lungs, harder breathing and potential trip to the hospital do not just affect her. Now she may not remember all that discomfort. That is her decision. What I do is let her know the part of that I personally do not want to have to deal with. I ask her if she wants to go to the hospital. She always answers, "No" and she makes a decision from that point. Her decision is usually to not eat the cheese, regardless of how much she loves the taste.

Is all of that a lot of work? YES. Who has the real power in the situation? Well, I maintain my power over the situation, because she usually will not eat the cheese. But my power comes from giving her the power to choose her fate. I do not have a desire to have power OVER HER as a person. I need power over the situation. There have been times where she chose her fate and it did not match what I wanted. So when the effect came and she was sniffling and coughing and carrying on, I simply looked at her and said, "So that cheese was good to you, huh?" My daughter looked at me and knew that what she was experiencing was a result of her own decision making. She seemed to be less dramatic once that point was brought to her attention. She handled the adverse effects much better. She took responsibility for what she created and got over it eventually. She made better decisions later on. My job was to not let it get out of hand. The life lesson was learned and I did not have to wear us both out with beating her for her to learn it.

Fear

It is pretty well known that F.E.A.R. can stand for False Evidence Appearing Real. Well, I know that for many of us, beating felt very real and created some real low feelings, both when we knew they were coming and when we actually received them. There was no thinking positively about it or making like the beating did not exist. We just knew that spanking was going to hurt—and it did!

I know that many beatings are given to create fear in a child. It is believed that if a young person is fearful enough of the beating or the threat of it, then he or she will not misbehave in the same way again.

My experience is that I actually never received a beating from my dad. My mom was the disciplinarian, but the fear we had was of my father, and there was no justified reason [for the fear] because, like I said, he never beat us. My mom put it all in our heads. "Wait until I tell your father! Your father's coming home! Don't do this! Don't do that! He has been working so hard!" She was a traditional mom and there were things she wanted in the house that I think she put on us. It all made us afraid of my father. But as we grew older and we began to talk to him, it wasn't him at all. He would scare us a little bit by raising his voice and telling us, "Don't do this! Don't do that!" He would pop the belt. He would bring us in the bathroom, sit on the tub and ask us what we did. We were already scared. Huffing and puffing and heaving, [we'd say] "I—don't—know—what—hap—pened." He would say "Be quiet!" and fold the belt in half and pop it and tell us to get out of there. We would run away crying. And that was it. But the fear really came from my mom and didn't stem from my father.

> **Vanessa T.M.**
> **After School Program Director,**
> **New York**

I want us to see fear as a PRESENCE in our homes. How does it feel? Is it an emotion you want to fill your home with? Is it an emotion you want to fill your child with? How do people act when they are fearful? Do these actions ever make situations better? One has to think of causing fear in another person. ❦ The time spent conjuring up a fear-filled plan can be better spent building something that will push the family forward.

Fear is unhealthy. It breeds insecurity and makes one feel physically weak. It is personally not an emotion I would want my child to have. I do not want that in her memory. I have no desire for my daughter to equate the emotion of fear with her mother. When my daughter thinks of her mom, I would like her to feel admiration. This, in turn, should help her trust me and make my job as a mom easier. I really do not know too many people who trust the people they fear. I have seen them want to block out the people they fear. I have seen them hate the people they fear. I have seen them cower before the people they fear. But I have seldom seen them willingly embrace the people they fear.

Non-Stop Love

Non-stop love means what we say does not always STOP our children from doing something. "Stop looking over there! Stop doing that! Stop, stop, stop, stop, stop." 🔑 Instead of stopping them from doing something, we can help them see how what they are doing can have an effect on their lives and the lives of the people around them.

🔑 If you want your daughter to stop dating a guy, then get an idea of what she really wants in a young man. See if her current interest in boys matches up to what she is. He should be a reflection of what she wants in herself. Have a conversation with both of them. If you want your child to stop playing near the electrical socket, explain the potential result of playing near the socket. It is not about teaching why YOU may fear electricity. It is about teaching the child about what electricity can do if not dealt with carefully. Show the child the purpose of the socket. Take away the mystery. Teach about safety. Show the child how to plug something in correctly.

🔑 If you want a child to stop at the light, teach the meaning of the light. See what the child already notices in that whole scene. Work with the child to make decisions based on what they know about the traffic light. Taking the time to help them make better decisions and not just respond to "stop" helps the child become a person who thinks and not just acts when told to do something. Like I said before, continually "stopping" young people makes adults who will not "go" to get anything. They get used to being told "stop." They get used to the idea that stopping will help them avoid trouble. No leader comes from this. You can get a child who acts like a robot from this, though.

The natural flow of things comes to a stop when being told to "stop" all the time. ☝ See if you, as an adult, can work within the natural flow of things—what happens naturally. It is much easier and gets rid of the panic. You just talk things through. It is not fear-based and does not make the child wrong for something he or she just may not know.

> *Whenever my children appear to be overwhelmed (that's the word I like to choose) by situations, I try to take things from them because I believe that it is the influence that they are dealing with. I just try to remove certain things from their lives. For example, if I let them go outside on the porch or something and one of them acts crazy or one of them does something that they are not taught to do, then they have to come in the house. If they do well on the porch, then they can go off the porch. They have parameters and distances they can go. The less they behave, the less likely they get to go that extra mile. The less exposure they'll get because of their actions. If they have problems with the set up that I created for them, then they will have less of a chance to explore more. Their exploration is shortened if they don't behave.*
>
> **Kandase K.**
> **Mother of six home-schooled children,**
> **Chicago**

Non-Stop Love

Stopping seems to bring some order, but the same order can be achieved by explaining and having a child make a choice through his or her own knowledge.

No Time Out

"Go sit in the corner and take a time out!" What is that? I know what it is, but, like a beating, it does not get to the root of the problem. Here, a child is told to "sit it out" until he or she gets over what made him or her upset in the first place. That child needs to feel involved and be allowed to bring something of his or her own to the table.

The challenge for me would be to get the child back to a pleasurable emotion so we could get back to work. One of the best ways I have dealt with situations that call for a "time out" in the past is to start everyday in class with a check in. I would always check in with the students and find out what their day was like or how they were feeling. Boy did they love this! It seems no one really cares enough to find out what is going on in a young person's day. I learned a lot!

One day, a seven year old student told me flat out that he was having a bad day. He said it was because his grandma spoke to him in the morning and she was rushing him. It was several hours later when I spoke to him, but he had been carrying that experience around with him and getting in trouble in school all day. No one thought to find out the "why."

Sometimes it does come from home. Sometimes I find out that the teacher's actions created the trouble. My students talk about the good things in their day, but during these sessions students express things they witnessed and

No Time Out

things they did not like and did not want to experience from their teachers. No one checks that out.

Being given a time out can make a young person feel degraded. Time out seems like a better alternative to yelling and hitting, but finding a preventative way to get to the real problem seems more effective.

I know. Who has the time to find out about all that is going on with a child? The time has to be made if we are concerned about who our children are becoming. I even ask my five-year-old daughter about her day. Sometimes she says "Not good." I listen and then we talk about some of the ways she can make it better. Sometimes I have to get involved, because the situation includes a teacher. Whatever it is, I do not respond with a blanket, "She has an attitude" or, "She is a problem." I attempt to find the problem so it can be fixed. My goal is to have a daughter whose mind is not preoccupied with negative things. Nothing good comes from those things. Plenty good comes out of her when she is happy and feeling good in her life.

Got Talk?

A lot of people try to downplay talking to children as a sign of weakness. I see it as the opposite. I see the ability to talk through a problem as a skill. Talking is how we get messages across in this culture. We can tell how the messages are received by the response we get, even when the response is non-verbal. If we say something that people misunderstand, eyebrows furrow and faces scrunch up. When people understand us, heads nod and sometimes a smile appears.

I disagree with the method of beating Black children. I believe that our children are here to learn from us. I believe our job is to teach our children. I don't believe that beating them is sending them the right message. I think they can learn more when you explain things to them thoroughly, so they can understand their options and what they are doing. I try to have a dialogue with them as much as possible. When we're out, I try to have an orientation with them so they can hear what's expected of them before we get out the car. Before I even move the car, I let them know what's expected of them. Before we go anywhere in public, I try to tell them what is expected of them. If they have good behavior, I try to tell them, "See how people respond to you? You see how people talk to you?" If they have bad behavior, I tell them, "Did you notice their expression or attitude toward you?" I point out how good behavior is more rewarding. It is more beneficial. They have more options. Respect people the way you like to be respected. Give people their space. And then when they (my children) decide to go against that, I try to allow them time to see how they affected the people that they were around and how they appeared or looked. I ask them how they felt about what people thought of them. Or, I ask them what they felt themselves.

**Kandase K.
Mother of six home-schooled children,
Chicago**

No matter how severe the problem, talking lends meaning to the situation. Most parents don't think about talking when a crisis or emergency arises, but this is when talking is needed the most. A person's ability to talk comes with the operation of the thinking mind, not the impulsive animalistic mind that beats other people. Thought usually comes before words are spoken. When words come out without much thought, they are usually hurtful.

When a child does something to displease an adult, it is the adult's job to get to the "why" behind the something. There is a reason behind why the child did what he or she did. Sometimes the reason points back to an action of the adult he or she is around. Adults do not want to look at that stuff, because it can point out some of our shortcomings. ❡If we admit to our shortcomings and communicate them to our children, then maybe we will get somewhere. Finding out how the child feels about a situation or even getting the child's feedback or advice can do wonders. Here again, young people have to be valued for this to work. They are more than little people to be ordered around. They definitely can contribute to the world they live in. And they ALWAYS have feelings about a situation. ❡ If we find out what their feelings are, then maybe we can create solutions that really help all the people involved.

All of this requires talking. There are various reasons why adults don't talk to young people. Some adults are genuinely afraid to talk to young people. Some are genuinely jealous of their children and cannot talk to them because of their jealousy. There has to be an effort to communicate in order to be understood, and we have to listen in order to learn. ♀ A key is to get off you for a moment and really get a child's input. Think about how you communicate with your child. Are you throwing up all over them with what you think and never listening? Are you too intense? Do you try to force teaching down their throats without looking and seeing what they are really interested in? Or are you REALLY listening to them? Balance it out, man! If we as parents listen, we can give children what they need based on who they are and what they want for themselves.

Communicating gets real answers. Talking takes out the assumptions and the guesswork. We just have to say what we mean, mean what we say and back it all up with some listening.

♀ Listen to what children say and, once they've spoken, be able to contribute some action to support what they said. If they said something hurtful, then talk about it. They need to think about what they said. Maybe they intended for what they said to hurt. If so, then find out why. If they say something good, let them know you heard it and how it made you feel. They need to hear that, too.

Got Talk?

Something is always behind what they say. Listening is the solution; it's the key to happiness on both sides.

The Look

What has no words, comes without warning, and stops children in their tracks? That's right, it is THE LOOK! You all know the look. I love the look! I think this is definitely a Black thing. We do it well and it works!

The look is usually very still, with no movement from the parent or the child. Sometimes the eyes may squint. Sometimes they open wide as we tighten our lips. There's no real blinking and it seems to stop children from doing whatever they should not be doing.

There is a lot of meaning in the look. The look can mean, "You betta' stop!" It can mean, "Ooooooo when I get to you..." It can mean whatever we want. I love it, because it is effective. When I give my daughter the look, her whole being changes. She looks back at me, stops her action and slows everything down. The look tells her I am not pleased with something. It works because I know my daughter ultimately does not want to see me upset.

The look is sudden. It can be a shocker! That's probably another reason why it works. With the look, a parent goes from being content to suddenly being upset. The child changes his or her behavior almost immediately and no one gets hit. I can get with that.

The look is something that has to be inherited. You have to be raised with the look. If you are not raised with the look, you will not know how to do the look. When you give children the look, there's nothing else you have to do. You look and it's like their world just freezes. They

The Look

start calling God and hope you are not going to get them. It's just an experience you have to inherit. Your child does something wrong and when they turn around you are just standing there and you give them the look. It's like the child knows that they have just messed up big time. They are wondering what's going to happen. But with the look, lo and behold, nothing has to happen. You just stand there and look at them for about five or ten seconds. They will not move. They will just stand there and look at you and you look back at them. You might ask if they understand and they may answer yes, but no words have really been spoken. The look can get you a long way.

Rick H.
Head of Maintenance, New York

The look is an instant discipliner. Kids do not want to get the look, and we can get some of what we want as parents with this secret weapon. Try not to laugh out loud the next time you use it, though. There is a smile hiding under there sometimes. And be prepared to still "skill up" as they get older. The look just may have a shelf life and may only work up to a certain age. I am not too sure, though. I am almost forty years old and I still know what my mama's "look" looks like.

Pleasure Moments

What are your pleasure moments? Describe them.

_____
_____
_____
_____
_____
_____
_____

It feels good thinking about them, right? Now what are the pleasure moments of our children? What makes them happy? Do we know?

Everybody loves pleasure moments. When something feels good, we smile. Sometimes we laugh. At times pleasure is spent with someone else. Some of us experience pleasure by relaxing by ourselves. It comes in all forms.

I have noticed that pleasure comes to children very easily. I have watched a paper clip become the item of pleasure and play. I have watched children enjoy skipping down the street. I have even seen them get joy from me saying "Hi" to them or asking them about their day. Children find pleasure in a lot of things.

I simply want a child's pleasure to be important to us as adults. I want to see my daughter happy and smiling, not pouting and mad. I have witnessed the joy of a four-year-old boy as he spoke with his dad at length on the

Pleasure Moments

train. And I have witnessed a child's joy shut down by an impatient adult who didn't want to hear anything the child had to say.

I carefully observe what brings my daughter joy and work to be sure she experiences pleasure as much as possible while she's in my care. When something brings her joy that I cannot give to her, we have a discussion about why I may not be able to give her that thing at that time, or how she can get it on her own. I make a point to notice her joy. I feel pleased when she's happy.

In the end, it is all about her experiences. I work with my daughter to manage things that bring her joy, like candy. A lot of candy can end in a stomach ache, rotten teeth or blotchy skin. Once we discuss the outcome of what pleases her, she makes a decision based on what she wants to experience. My job is to keep her happily living this life until she takes charge of it. I want to create a person that seeks to have joy in her life and who creates pleasure moments for herself and others as she grows.

I had many pleasure moments growing up. I read songs from the record sleeves with my mother and brother. My brother and I used to dance in the mirror with my mother and make award-winning school projects with her. She made sure we had the latest video games. We never felt a need to be out of the house to find pleasure.

While our parenting will come with its challenges, it is important to give thought to living with pleasure. As parents, we have the power to create pleasure for ourselves and our children. ♀ All we have to do is tap into everyone's likes and create the magic from there. It takes time, but it may not be hard to do at all.

PLEASURE UP PEOPLE!

What Do They Want?

Listen. She's crying and crying. She's asking and asking. He's tugging and tugging and tugging. All of these are common ways young people try to communicate. They may even scream out loud!

I've heard kids ask about everything from the sky to the street, from a person to a piece of food. They always want to say something or know something. "Shut up already!" or "Not now!" have been some of the common responses I have heard from parents. I have even witnessed an occasional pop on the behind or leg when a child wants to look out the window or stand holding the pole on the train.

Well, what do children want? If you find that out, the frustration that prompts you to strike kids will probably go away. Crying usually means hunger, pain or discomfort when the child can't speak. Asking questions is how a child learns the workings of the world and how to operate in it. Tugging at clothes sometimes is the only way to get an adult to listen, because no one is paying the child any attention.

As adults, we need to learn to talk young people's talk. We have to hear their voices and points of view as something valuable and worth hearing. It is really no different than learning about a potential client or a possible mate and saying things that relate to their lives. This is how we get them to listen up. Answering questions and giving young people the conversations they want can solve many problems. Sometimes it is just about making them the food they want, when they want it. It IS okay for them to WANT. There's no rule that says that being young means NOT getting the things you want. Wanting something and actually getting it creates a good feeling. Parents spend a lot of time stopping young people from getting what they want. There is not always a lesson in making sure young people DON'T get what they want when they want it. The thing to look at is whether what they are asking for is really all that big in the scheme of things. I have found that young people don't really want much.

Well, I am basically old school. I don't go by the concept grandmothers or mothers did as far as spanking to get a point across. That came from a slave mentality and a lot of our kids still have social and behavioral problems from that. It is a post traumatic slavery syndrome type of sickness.

I am used to the old school raising children on a mental level: stimulating their minds and being able to relate to get their time and to understand whatever they want in life. They can be whatever they want to be and they can be observant. They can make choices and they can be in control of their destinies, as long as they know themselves and their Creator. They can get to their next destination or level and be whatever they want to be. We have to help them realize they can learn at all levels. They have to understand how much more they want out of life. That is what I try to relay to the kids. I don't understand the stuff about beating them, because I can look at you a certain way and give you a straight up stare down and you would know that I'm not havin' it (as far as doing something wrong). We can

What Do They Want?

communicate to where it is stimulating to the mind. We will come to an understanding so that we're on the same program and being respectful.

Malik M., Senior Broker, New York

We seem to have some issues as a people when it comes to having things. We figure if we do not need something as adults, then our children should not want it as children. This is not about just providing material things. Sometimes it is, but most often it is just about checking our children's emotions. Is having a particular thing going to bring them joy? Are they sad because they can't have something? How our children feel will usually determine how they act in life. Often, they only want acknowledgement or a little time from us. Those things do not cost us anything, but they will require a bit of patience from us. Giving patience and time can make all the loving difference in the world.

Love to Hear Them Laugh

There is nothing like a child's laugh. How can a being so small make such loud noise? I know how, but that is another book. If you listen to that sound, really listen to the pitch, the rhythm and the intensity, you will find it very pleasing.

I am always curious about what children could possibly find so funny. I always want to know the cause. What has the power to bring the laugh out of them? A child's laughter signals he or she is in a happy place. If I see a violent act creating laughter, I address it. But most times the laughter comes from a sound, a look, or it is a contagious laughter stemming from someone else's laughter. Whatever it is, it is good to hear and see.

A child's smile is healing. It is a signal that all things are good in his or her world. It usually means a child is feeling some kind of freedom. Work not to interrupt that joy the next time you hear it. Or, better yet, try creating a child's laughter. Now THAT is a skill! Being able to make a child smile and laugh is a great feeling for both the adult and the child. Can you do it? Listen and watch for the things that bring laughter out of children. You might be surprised. Sometimes it is just you and the fact that you allowed yourself to come into their world.

__Let 'Em Live__

I dedicate this chapter to Mama Gail, who said to me, "We just have to let them live." Our children are here to explore their own worlds. Everything they do is an extension of something: how a teacher acts, what they see in the street or, perhaps, who they were in another life. Who is to know? Sometimes I do not know. But I am keen enough to talk to young people and find out. Rest in Sweet Peace Mama Gail!

When children run and spin and experiment and touch and ask questions and watch and yell and on and on, they are just living. They are functioning in the world the way they know how. We can impact this with how we act. Check what they see from us. One of the keys is to not spaz out when they are doing something we might not do as adults. Children do a lot of what they do to get a response from a friend or an adult. So how about talking with them about how their actions affect the people around them? My daughter has copied some of my behaviors and they are cool around me, but maybe not in public. For example, one day I told her that when she exclaimed, "Oh Jeeesus!," it was understandable to me, but may not have been fully understood or liked by some other people around her. I never told her she was wrong. I only asked her to be aware of her surroundings when she chooses to say those words. I think I even noticed a little volume control from her when

Let 'Em Live

she said it after our little discussion. She is a wise ole five year old.

> *My theory is to let kids live! Let them do their own thing. Don't chastise them, don't point the finger, compliment them. Pull them to the side when they are doing something wrong. Give them positive feedback. Let little girls go out and explore their lives. Just let them know what's happening out there. Don't hold them too tight. If you hold them too tight, then when they get out there, they are going to run rampant! Let them be little girls and tell them everything that is going on.*
>
> *It's not always about pointing the finger at them. Sometimes kids act bad for a reason. Sometimes it's not the kids, it's the parents. What are the parents telling the kids? How is the household? What are they doing in the household? How are they living over there? That reflects on the kids. It's not the kids all the time. So stop pointing the finger at them.*
>
> **Mama Gail**
> **Caterer and Top Chef, New York**

Letting our children live eases their tension. Watch them and guide them in a good direction. If we control their every word and every move, they seem to become like robots. They don't have their own ideas about things. They are easily controlled and can create trouble for themselves and others. If they can think for themselves and tell us their opinions, they can usually contribute more to the world and have greater confidence in themselves.

Create It

Who our children are now and who they will become are byproducts of our life experiences and theirs. That is how I see it. Yes our children come here with their own purposes to do their own things on this earth. The real deal is that they can struggle at becoming what we design or we can help them along. The "no pain no gain" choice can end up a dozen different ways, because we usually do not think through making a person struggle. The struggling usually comes from poor decisions, dreams deferred, drugs, beating, yelling, negative input, etc. The pain usually comes because no one thought about how to make life easier. Our children can still have a good game of life and the things they want. This does not require that we do things for them. They can actually make their own decisions, earn what they get, have fun and grow.

As a parent you are supposed to teach your kids right from wrong and get them in the right direction. You allow them to make their mistakes, because they are misguided in ways. They are going to make their mistakes in life. But it is up to you to choose to help them choose the right path. You cannot force anything on them. If you have a dream and a passion that you never finished in your life, you can't force your dream on your child. For example, if you wanted to play music but the child does not want to play music, you can't force that child to play the piano or the trumpet or something that you weren't able to play when you were a child. That becomes a forced hobby. You can't allow your child to be in a situation like that, trying to live

Create It

your dream. As a parent you just have to teach your kids the positive things in life and hopefully they'll come up the right way.

You have to keep them in a lot of programs. You know, keep them interested in different subjects. Let them explore the world. There are fifty states and a whole bunch of countries. They don't have to stay in the same state. They can explore different states and maybe be an exchange student in another country and learn a different language. They don't have to stay where they live. As they get older they learn more by exploring the world. You want your kids to expand their minds.

Brian G., Computer Technician, New York

It is about them being good at something. Although children are not in charge of their lives in the beginning, someone needs to actually see that they have a good life game to play and decide to give them some powers to use. Can they bake? Are they interested in acting? Do they love food? Are they talkers? Can they dance? Are they great artists? As parents we can watch and find ways to make them better at what they do. If a child is getting in trouble in school because he or she is talking all the time, then maybe your child is an orator or a debater. Find a topic the child is really interested in and have him or her go out and talk about it. Maybe the child loves music. Find out if the child wants to write it, produce it, sing or play an instrument. If you cannot afford the things your child needs, cool! Find an organization that will help. Let the children show what they know and let the world sing their praises. Get them where they have to go.

Create It

Are they exceptionally good at flipping and doing cartwheels? Good! Find that flipping institute or the circus or something. Create the opportunity for them. Just create it! Set the stage for the life that makes them happy and prosperous. This is how we can populate the world with good, powerful people. This will make our lives less strenuous and more meaningful. We may not have lived all of our dreams; let's do what we can as parents to foster the dreams of our children. I am not talking about what WE want them to do. I am talking about what THEY want to do. Sometimes it is the same as what we want and sometimes it is not. Either way, we just have to be observant and give them the opportunity to work toward their own dreams.

Let's get them to prosper and not hold them back. To beat them is to lower their value. Treat them well and work on your own ability to handle all your family situations with understanding and without violence. Everyone will be better for it.

Glossary

ability (n.) – the physical, mental, financial, or legal power to accomplish something

abuse (n.) – bad or improper treatment; maltreatment

abusive (adj.) – using, containing, or characterized by harshly or coarsely insulting language

account (n.) – reason ; basis

acknowledge (v.) – to show or express that you recognize something or realization of it

address (v.) – to deal with or discuss

adverse (adj.) – harmful or unfavorable

aggressive (adj.) – inclined to behave in an actively hostile way

allude (v.) – - To make an indirect reference to something

appearing (v.) – seeming; looking like

assumption (n.) – Something taken without question or accepted as true without question or proof

atrocious (adj.) – extremely or shockingly wicked, cruel, or brutal

being (n.) – a human being; person

being (n.) – one's basic or essential nature; personality.

had better (idiom) - , would be wiser or more well-advised to; ought to:

bitter (adj.) – marked by resentment

cater (v.) – to attend to the wants or needs of

charge (n.) – care or custody

Glossary

charge, in (idiom) – in command; having supervisory power

citizen (n.) – a resident of a city or town, especially one entitled to enjoy privileges there

clinical (adj.) – of, relating to, or connected with a clinic

compatible (adj.) – capable of existing or living together in harmony

confide (v.) – to have full trust; have faith

conjuring (v.) – creating anew, especially by means of the imagination

conscience (n.) – the part of the mind made up of material of which the individual is aware

consciously (adv.) – with knowledge of one's own mental operations or actions

consistency (n.) – the condition of sticking to the same principles, course, or form

contagious (adj.) – tending to spread from person to person

contribution (n.) – that which is given

corporal punishment (n.) – physical punishment, such as spanking, inflicted on a child by an adult in authority

cower (v.) – to cringe or crouch in fear or shame

critical (adj.) – tending to find fault or to judge with harshness, often too quickly

crucial (adj.) – involving an extremely important decision or result

deal (v.) – to be able to handle competently or successfully

deferred (adj.) – postponed or delayed

degraded (adj.) – reduced in quality or value

Glossary

detriment (n.) – loss, damage, disadvantage, or injury

effects (n.) – things brought about by a cause; results

embrace (v.) – to hug or hold close with the arms, usually as an expression of affection

emphasize (v.) – to stress a point

encouragement (n.) – that which serves to support, promote, or advance; that which can serve as an incentive and increase of confidence when given

energy (n.) – the habit of energetic, forceful activity

ensure (v.) – to make sure or certain

equate (v.) – to consider or treat as equal or equivalent

esoteric (adj.) – understood by or meant for only the select few who have special knowledge or interest

evidence (n.) – something that makes plain or clear; a sign

fate (n.) – a final result or consequence; an outcome

fear (n.) – the feeling or condition of being afraid; an emotion stirred up by danger, evil, pain, etc. that is about to happen

feedback (n.) – a reaction or response to a particular process or activity

foresight (n.) – an act of looking forward

foster (n.) – to promote the growth or development of; encourage

free (adj.) – able to do something with the power of choosing one's own actions

freedom (n.) – the right to enjoy all the privileges or special rights of citizenship, membership, etc. in a community

Glossary

furrow (v.) – to make wrinkles in one's face

future (n.) – something that will exist or happen in time to come

genuinely (adv.) – authentic; real

gracious (interjection) – used as an exclamation of surprise, relief, or dismay

halt (v.) – to cause to stop temporarily or permanently; bring to a stop

handling (v.) – managing, dealing with, or being responsible

harbor (v.) – to keep or hold in the mind; maintain; entertain

havoc (n.) – disorder or chaos

imbalanced (adj.) – a lack of being in harmony

immune (adj.) – not responsive

impact (v.) – to have an effect on; influence

impulsive (adj.) – inclined to act quickly and hastily rather than with thought

indoctrinated (adj.) – programmed, as with feelings and opinions with a specific bias, belief or point of view

input (n.) – contribution of information, ideas, or opinions

instinctively (adv.) – arising from impulse; spontaneous and unthinking

intangible (adj.) – not able to be touched

intention (n.) – purpose or attitude leading to one's actions or conduct

intently (adv.) – having the attention sharply focused or fixed on something

Glossary

introverted (adj.) – concerned primarily with one's own thoughts and feelings; shy

invalidation (n.) – something weakened or made valueless

irk (v.) – to irritate, annoy

jewels (n.) – people or things that are treasured, esteemed, or absolutely necessary or essential

justifications (n.) – reasons or explanations that defend actions, beliefs, etc.

keen (adj.) – having or showing great mental penetration

kinks (n.) – flaws or imperfections likely to hold back the successful operation of something, like in a plan

lapse (n.) – a passage of time

life (n.) – the interval of time between birth and death

literally (adv.) - actually; without exaggeration

mate (n.) – one who customarily associates with another; a companion

material (n.) – relating to, concerned with, or involving physical things

misdeed (n.) – an evil or wicked action

momentarily (adv.) – a short period of time; briefly

muster (v.) – to assemble or gather

negate (v.) – to make ineffective or invalid

no avail (phr.) - no use; ineffective

notion (n.) – a mental image or representation; an idea

observant (adj.) – taking notice; viewing or noticing attentively; watchful; attentive

orator (n.) – a public speaker

Glossary

panic (n.) – sudden overwhelming fear, with or without cause, that produces hysterical or irrational behavior and often spreads quickly

parent (n.) – one who gives birth to or nurtures and raises a child; usually a father or mother

peers (n.) – people who are equal to another in abilities, qualifications, age, background, or social status

phenomenon (n.) – an observable fact or event

pitch (n.) – the degree of height or deepness of a tone or of sound

pleasure (n.) – enjoyment or satisfaction derived from what is to one's liking; gratification; delight

potential (adj.) – capable of being or becoming

preventative (adj.) – carried out to turn away expected hostile or destructive behavior or actions

prompt (v..) – to move to act

pull our coat tails (idiom) – make aware

putrid (adj.) – in a state of foul decay or decomposition, as animal or vegetable matter; rotten

rampant (adj.) – unchecked; unrestrained

rationalize (v.) – to devise self-satisfying but incorrect reasons for (one's behavior)

reason (v.) – think logically

reason (n.) – the basis or motive for an action or decision

reflect (v) – to think, ponder, or meditate

remote (n.) – a device used to control the operation of an apparatus or machine, as a television set, from a distance

resentment (n.) – strong displeasure; anger; hostility stirred up by a wrong experienced

Glossary

resort (v.) – to turn to for aid or relief

resource (n.) – something that can be used for support or help

response (n.) – an answer or reply, as in words or in some action

right (adv.) – – 1. exactly; precisely (pgs.11, 54) 2. immediately; promptly (pg.11)

right (n.) – 1. a true statement; freedom from error or falsehood; adherence to truth or fact (pg. 12) 2. something that is due to a person by law, tradition, or nature (pg. 13, 36)

right (adj.) – correct in judgment, opinion, or action (pgs. 15, 16, 42, 59, 74)

root (n.) – the source or origin of a thing

run-of-the-mill (adj.) – not special or outstanding; average

sacrifice (n.) – the act of giving up something highly valued for the sake of something considered to have a greater value

scrunch (v.) – make wrinkles or creases on a smooth surface

severity (n.) – intense harshness

shortcomings (n.) – failures, defects, or deficiencies in conduct, condition, thought, ability, etc.

spaz (v.) – to become extremely emotional; to lose control

squint (v.) – to look with the eyes partly closed

state (n.) – the condition of a person or thing, as with respect to circumstances or attributes

strenuous (adj.) – requiring great effort, energy, or exertion

Glossary

subject (adj.) – being in a position that places one under the power or authority of another or others

succumb (v.) – buckle under, give in

shelf life (n.) – the term or period during which a product remains effective, useful, or suitable for consumption

tactic (n.) – a plan or procedure for promoting a desired end or result

tone (n.) – a particular quality or way of sounding, of the voice expressive of some meaning, feeling, spirit, etc.

tone (n.) – a particular mental state or disposition; spirit, character

underlying (adj.) – discoverable only by a close examination

up (v. tr.) – to increase (pg. 58)

valid (adj.) – founded in truth; capable of being justified, defended, or supported

validate (v.) – to make sufficient in strength or force; to make capable of being justified, defended, or supported; to make sound; good

various (adj.) – different kinds or forms

verification (n.) – evidence that confirms the truth of something

voice (n.) – the right to present and receive consideration of one's desires or opinions

warrant (v.) – to give reason or justify

welts (n.) – ridges on the surface of the body, as from a blow of a stick or whip

whack (adj.) slang – not good

Glossary

willingly (adv.) – - Done, given or accepted, voluntarily or without a problem

Author Bio

Mother of one child, but considered a mother to many, Asadah Kirkland, more affectionately known as "Ms. K," has been working with kids for over fifteen years. Working in unconventional classroom settings allowed Asadah the freedom to teach her own curricula and deliver her own messages that catered to the uplifting of her students. Her work with young people involved teaching and working intently to solve problems within their families, while her courses kept life fun and encouraged them to do their best. Asadah's expertise, planning and troubleshooting helped in developing and raising her five-year old daughter and her brand of motherhood stems from her practice as a good educator.

Beating Black Kids is Asadah's first published book and is designed to encourage better actions and decision making amongst her parental peers. This book is the sum total of her observations, practice and experience as an

Author Bio

educator. What the book brings to the forefront is based on real life. It is not meant to be theoretical or clinical.

Beating Black Kids is challenging. People can read Asadah's words and view their own behavior. Asadah's goal is not to point the finger, but to offer solutions. The solutions, if valued, should help Black parents make decisions for the greater good. *Beating Black Kids* is Asadah's contribution to making this world more enjoyable, starting with less stress in the family.